MW00679772

To

_____

From

_____

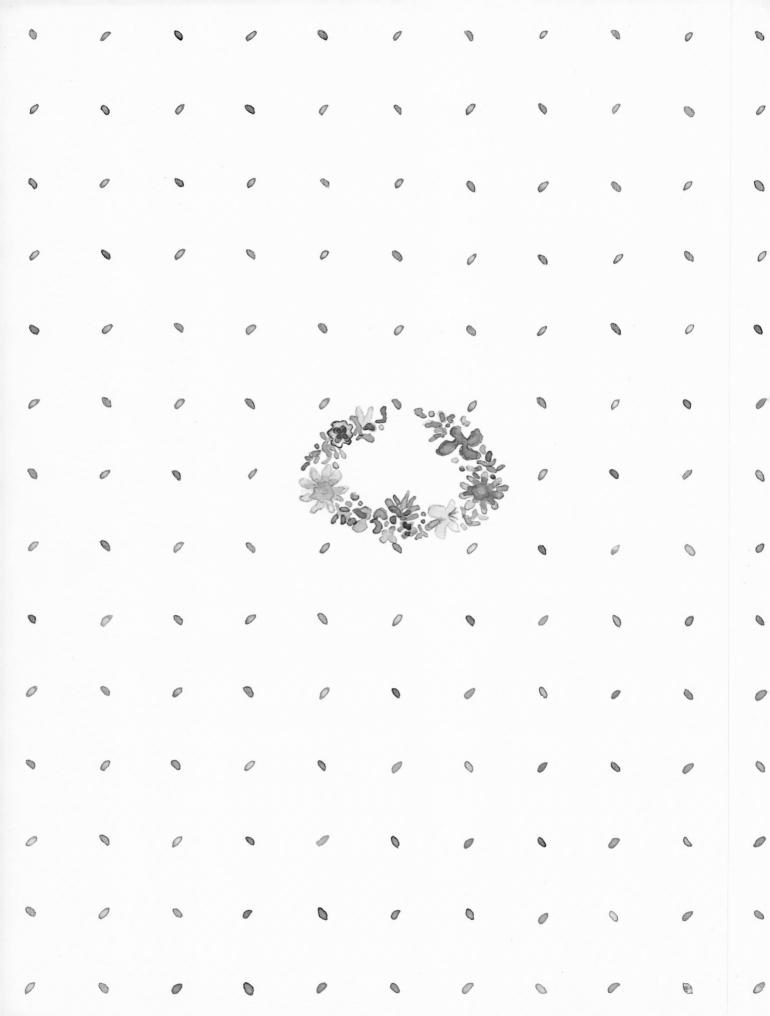

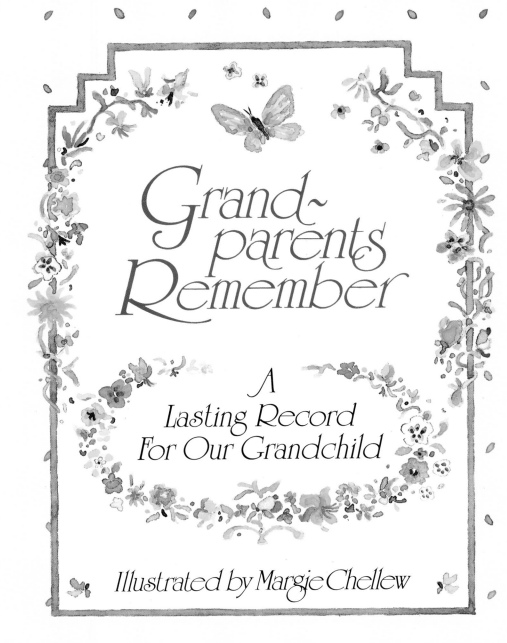

Grand~parents Remember

A
Lasting Record
For Our Grandchild

Illustrated by Margie Chellew

MEMORY PRESS

MEMORY PRESS

351 Whitehorse Road
Balwyn Victoria 3103 Australia
A.C.N. 005 966 245

First Published 1991
Reprinted 1992
Illustrations and design © The Five Mile Press Pty Ltd

Illustrations by Margie Chellew
Design by Geoff Hocking
Typeset by DigiType

ISBN 0 86788 275 1

Printed and Bound in China

Introduction

Important details of your family history can easily be lost and forgotten unless you make a conscious effort to write them down. This book will help you set out your wealth of recollections in a logical and readable format.

When you have filled it in, it will become much more than a decorative and entertaining gift — it will be a unique collection of personal memories, and an invaluable record about your family. In time, it may even become a treasured heirloom to be passed down from generation to generation.

So fill it in with love and care, and add as many favourite photographs, family mementoes and interesting documents as you can. This is a very special gift — not just for your grandchild, but for future generations of your family.

Contents

Contents

Your Mother's Family Tree

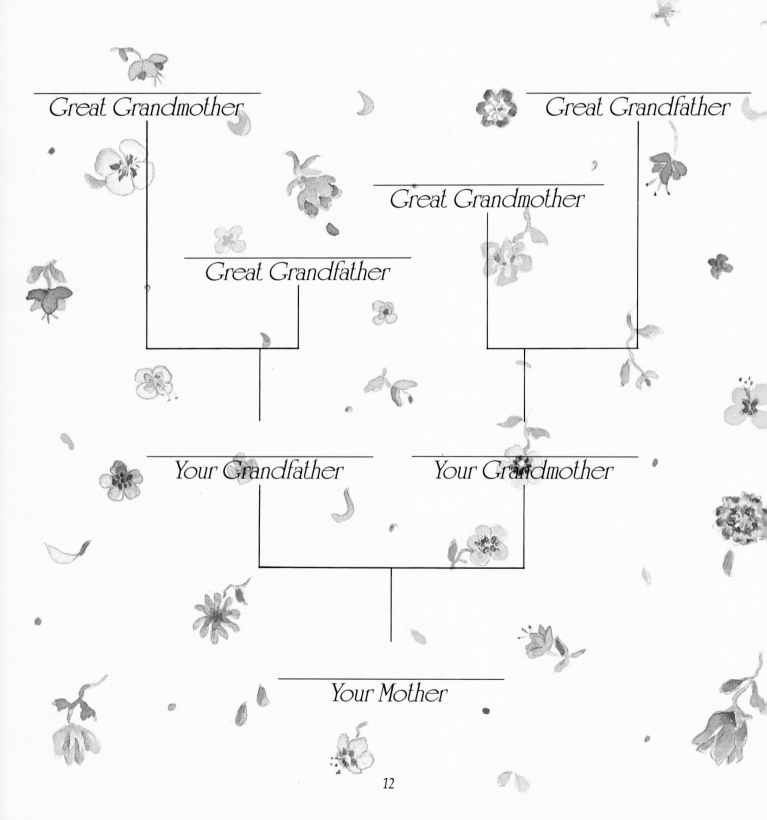

Great Grandmother

Great Grandfather

Great Grandmother

Great Grandfather

Your Grandfather

Your Grandmother

Your Mother

Your Father's Family Tree

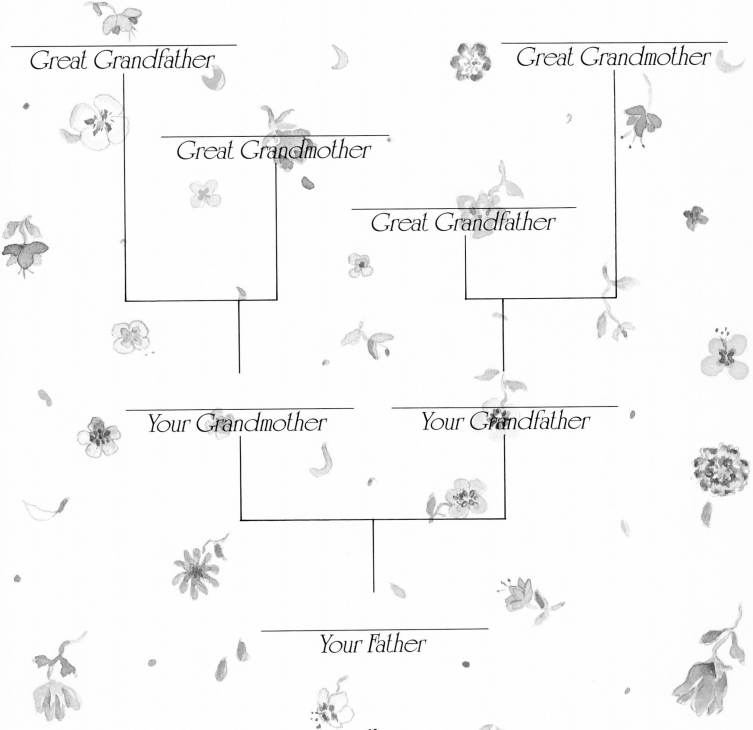

Great Grandfather

Great Grandmother

Great Grandmother

Great Grandfather

Your Grandmother

Your Grandfather

Your Father

"Grandmother"

Arabic: Sitt
Bulgarian: Baba
Chinese: Zu-mu
Danish: Farmor, Mormor
Dutch: Oma
English: Grandmother, Grandma
Grandmama, Granny
Nana, Nanny
Fiji: Bu
Finnish: Isoäiti, Mummi
French: Grand-mère
German: Grossmutter
Greek: Yiayia
Hawaiian: Kupuna wahine, Tutu
Hebrew: Savta
Hungarian: Nagyanana
Irish: Mama, Seanmháthair
Italian: Nonna
Japanese: Oba-San
Koori: Bargi, Bakkano, Maiyanowe
Korean: Hal Mo-ni
Maori: Kuia
Norwegian: Farmor, Mormor
Papua New Guinean: Lapun Mama, Tumbuna
Polish: Babcia
Portuguese: Avó
Romanian: Bunica
Russian: Babushka
Spanish: Abuela, Abuelita
Swedish: Farmor, Mormor
Thai: Yai, Taa
Turkish: Büyük anne
Vietnamese: Bà
Welsh: Mam-gu, Nain
Yiddish: Bobe

"Grandfather"

Arabic: Jad
Bulgarian: Dyado
Chinese: Yeye, Zufu
Danish: Morfar, Farfar
Dutch: Grootvader, Opa
English: Grandfather, Grandpa
Grandad, Gramps
Fiji: Tai
Finnish: Isoisä
French: Grand-père
German: Grossvater
Greek: Papous
Hawaiian: Kupuna kane
Hebrew: Saba
Hungarian: Nagyapa
Irish: Seanathair
Italian: Nonno
Japanese: Ojíi-san
Koori: Nerbungeron, Ngaityapalle,
Pola, Tipi, Ulwai
Korean: Harabugi
Maori: Koroua
Norwegian: Bestefar
Papua New Guinean: Lapun Papa, Tumbuna
Polish: Dziadek
Portuguese: Avô
Romanian: Bunic
Russian: Dyedushka
Spanish: Abuelo
Swedish: Morfar, Farfar
Thai: Yaa, Poo
Turkish: Dede
Vietnamese: Ông
Welsh: Tad-cu
Yiddish: Zayde

Grandmother's Grandparents
MATERNAL

My Grandfather's Name

_____

_____

My Grandmother's Name

_____

_____

My Grandparents Met

_____

_____

They Were Married

When _____

Where _____

_____

They Lived At

_____

_____

My Grandfather Earned His Living

_____

_____

_____

Grandmother's Grandparents
PATERNAL

My Grandfather's Name

My Grandmother's Name

My Grandparents Met

They Were Married

When   Where

They Lived At

My Grandfather Earned His Living

Grandfather's Grandparents
MATERNAL

My Grandfather's Name

_____

_____

My Grandmother's Name

_____

_____

My Grandparents Met

_____

_____

They Were Married

When _____ Where _____

They Lived At

_____

_____

My Grandfather Earned His Living

_____

_____

_____

Grandfather's Grandparents
PATERNAL

My Grandfather's Name

_____

_____

My Grandmother's Name

_____

_____

My Grandparents Met

_____

_____

They Were Married

When   Where

_____

They Lived At

_____

_____

My Grandfather Earned His Living

_____

_____

_____

Grandmother's Parents

My Father's Name

My Mother's Name

My Parents Met

My Father's Work

My Mother's Work

Grandfather's Parents

My Father's Name

My Mother's Name

My Parents Met

My Father's Work

My Mother's Work

Where Grandmother Was Born

Place Photo Here

_____ *I Was Born* _____

When   Where

I Was Named _____

I Weighed _____

_____

Where Grandfather Was Born

Place Photo Here

I Was Born

When   *Where*

I Was Named

I Weighed

As A Girl

Place Photo Here

My Family Lived

I Went to School

My Ambition

Favourite Things

Song _____

Movie _____ Actor _____

Actress _____ Book _____

_____

_____

_____

_____

_____

_____

_____

_____

_____

_____

_____

_____

As A Boy

Place Photo Here

My Family Lived

I Went to School

My Ambition

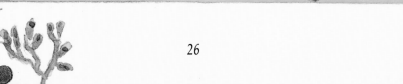

Favourite Things

Song _____

Movie _____   Actor _____

Actress _____   Book _____

_____

_____

_____

_____

_____

_____

_____

_____

_____

_____

_____

_____

_____

As A Young Woman
FAVOURITE THINGS

Place Photo Here

_____

_____

_____

_____

_____

As A Young Man
FAVOURITE THINGS

Place Photo Here

Our Engagement

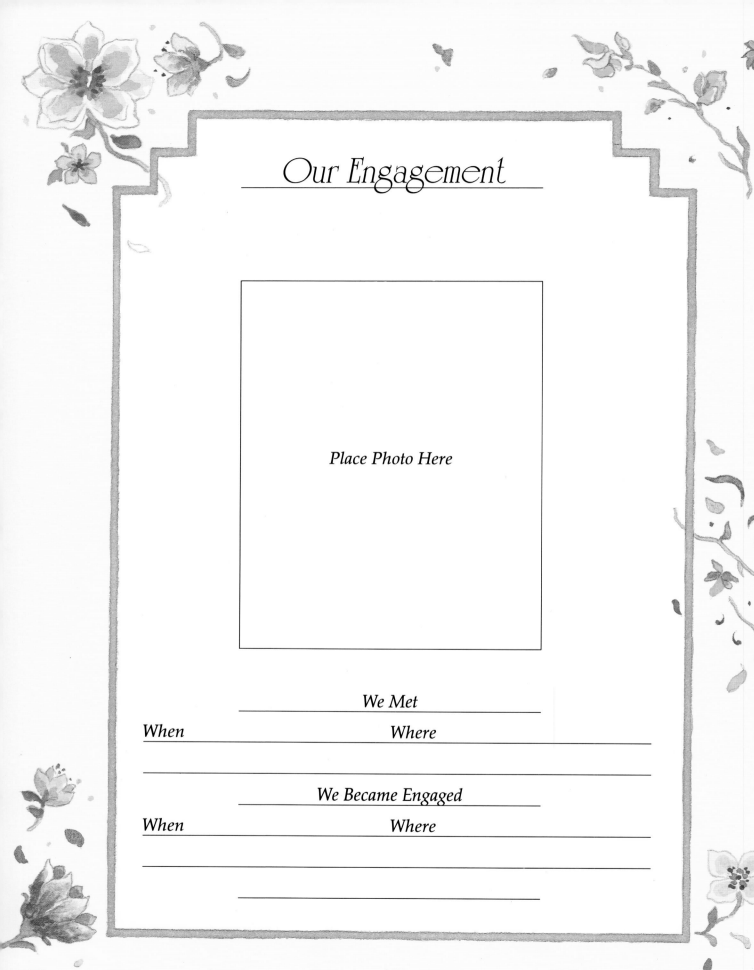

Place Photo Here

We Met

When   Where

We Became Engaged

When   Where

*Place
Memento
Here*

Our Wedding Day

We Were Married

Date   *Time*

Place

We Celebrated By

_____

_____

Grandmother Wore

_____

_____

A Memorable Gift

_____

_____

Our Most Vivid Memory

_____

_____

Our Honeymoon

_____

_____

_____

Place Photo Here

33

Our First Year Of Marriage

We First Lived At

_____

_____

Our Fondest Memory

_____

_____

Grandfather's Job Was

_____

_____

Grandmother's Job Was

_____

_____

We Enjoyed

_____

_____

_____

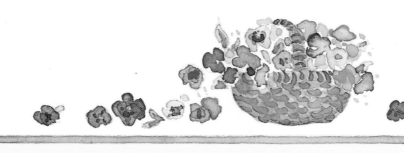

Our First Year Of Marriage

Place Photo Here

Our Child Was Born

Our Child Was Born

When _____ Where _____

We Lived At _____

We Named Our Child

Full Name _____

We Chose That Name Because _____

_____

Colour Of Eyes _____ Colour Of Hair _____

Weight _____ First Word _____

Favourite Toys

_____

_____

Favourite Games

_____

_____

When I Think About The Time

_____

_____

_____

Our Child Was Born

Place Photo Here

Our Child Growing Up

At School

Best Subjects

Showed Talent In

Ambitions

Hobbies

Sports

Our Child Growing Up

_____

Place Photo Here	*Place Photo Here*

_____

Our Child's Teenage Years

Favourite Music

_____

_____

Favourite Sports

_____

_____

Major Interests

_____

_____

We Were Strict About

_____

_____

We Were Proud That

_____

_____

What We Remember Most

_____

_____

Our Child's Teenage Years

Place Photo Here

_____

_____

_____

_____

_____

Your Parents

They Met

How _____

_____

_____

When _____

Where _____

They Were Married

Date _____

Place _____

Your Father Worked As

_____

_____

Your Mother Worked As

_____

_____

_____

Place Photo Here

Your Birth

You Were Born

When _____   Where _____

You Weighed _____

We Thought You Resembled

_____

_____

Your Star Sign

_____

_____

You Were Given The Name

_____

Because _____

_____

_____

_____

_____

Your Birth

Place Photo Here

Our Earliest Memories Of You

We Remember When You . . .

Place Photo Here

Our Earliest Memories Of You

_____

_____

_____

_____

_____

_____

_____

_____

_____

_____

_____

_____

_____

_____

_____

Our Earliest Memories Of You

Our Earliest Memories Of You

Place Photo Here

_____

_____

_____

_____

Family Reunions

Our Family Gets Together

Place Photo Here

Family Reunions

Our Family

_____   _____
_____   _____
_____   _____
_____   _____
_____   _____
_____   _____
_____   _____
_____   _____
_____   _____
_____   _____
_____   _____
_____   _____
_____   _____
_____   _____
_____   _____

Family Holidays

We Like To Go To

_____

_____

_____

_____

_____

_____

_____

Special Holidays We Shared

_____

_____

_____

Family Heirlooms

_____

_____

_____

_____

_____

_____

_____

_____

_____

_____

_____

Favourite Relatives

Favourite Relatives

_____

_____

_____

_____

Place Photo Here

Place Photo Here

Place Photo Here

Place Photo Here

Place Photo Here

Our Special Memories

We Want You To Know That

_____

_____

_____

_____

_____

_____

_____

_____

_____

_____

_____

Mementoes

Place Favourite Photos
Newspaper Clippings, Mementoes
Here

Mementoes

*Place Favourite Photos
Newspaper Clippings, Mementoes
Here*

Mementoes

Place Favourite Photos
Newspaper Clippings, Mementoes
Here